The Ark of
Newark

and Other Poems

by

DAVID GALLER

Crane & Hopper
2020

Copyright © 2020 by David Galler

All rights reserved. No part of this book may be reproduced or transmitted in any form or by any means, electronic or mechanical, including photocopying, recording or by any information storage or retrieval system, without permission in writing from the Publisher, with the exception of short quotation in review and critical articles.

Crane & Hopper
100 Ardsley Avenue West
PO Box 78
Ardsley-on-Hudson, NY 10503-0078
USA

ISBN: 978-1-951121-27-3

VERSE COLLECTIONS
BY DAVID GALLER

The Ark of Newark and Other Poems   2020

Twenty-Two Poems   2019

A Time in Eternity   2007

Soliloquies   2004

Edward Thomas's Gun   2001

Collected Poems   1995

Third Poems   1979

Leopards in the Temple   1968

Walls and Distances   1959

The distance that separates feeling from words... the moment I try to speak, not only do I fail to express what I am feeling, but what I am feeling slowly transforms itself into what I am saying. Or at least what makes me act is certainly not what I am feeling but what I am saying.

— Clarice Lispector
from *Near to the Wild Heart*

To write regular verse... destroys an infinite number of fine possibilities, but at the same time it suggests a multitude of distant and totally unexpected thoughts.

— Paul Valéry

CONTENTS

PEACE ... 11

A PRINCE ... 12

THE LAUGH ... 14

PRECOCITY ... 16

1940s: HIPSTERS ON A WINTER NIGHT ... 17

OLD-TIMERS ... 18

LYRIC ... 19

FOR BARACK OBAMA, 44TH U.S. PRESIDENT ... 20

PHILOKTETES II ... 23

THE ANGEL ... 24

INGRES ... 26

MUNCH ... 32

ARSHILE GORKY ... 38

LESTER YOUNG ... 41

FALLING ... 50

A COMFORTER ... 52

A WORKPLACE ... 53

A FAREWELL ... 54

THE ARK OF NEWARK ... 56

JUDAS AHASVERUS ... 58

THE PRISONER POET ... 62

EVENINGS WITH HOWARD NEMEROV, 1960 ... 64

MEMORY OF TED WEISS RETIRED IN PRINCETON ... 66

SONG OF DECLINE ... 67

DIMINISHMENT ... 68

GETTING IT RIGHT ... 69

GONESBERG ... 70

AND THEN ... 71

I.M. Thelma

*Who in her lifetime offered as much care,
worldliness, and inspiration as one could hope for*

PEACE

for Nikki and Herb

With body, mind, and the
Imagination even,
Each at rest, and we,
It follows, painlessly riven
By that greatest rarity
Of tension-free, undriven
Waiting, with charity
Of lacking any given
Object, ourselves not subject
Consciously, benefaction
Though it be, or thief,
Peace is the infraction
Of our very days: its project
Hungered after, though brief.

A PRINCE

Who was I, when, maybe five or six,
Fed up, if that is the word for such a time,
With kin and their companions garrulous and high at their country
                                                                garden
Party, I chose to climb

An old path, hardly visible under branches,
Up through grasses toward a wood I'd been
Warned often not to enter where, figure ungovernable as
A cloud, I passed on in.

At once, into lulling half-darkness, tall trees
That barred the sun out opened into, a dreamt sash,
Invisible, 'round my waist, which through sighing thickets and tugged
                                                                branches
You would have thought would lash

Mercilessly, but ushered in then on sudden
Sun-washed clearings broken by birdcalls, so
I never thought of stretches forgotten to reach them, but, after
Some time felt the glow

Of sheer fatigue, and who was I? I asked
But he who made a pallet of leaves as if
He did this every night, and slept, dreamless, until
Dawn's glow, to wake and sniff;

Aware at a stone's throw of a large white horse,
Agèd yet patient, pawing the ground;
And who was I, again, but he who followed –
This magic made no sound

As off through the trees he slowly trailed ahead
Soon as I'd risen, out from that far, lost place
Finally, back through grasses to a house bristling with parents and
                                                                                   guests

Predictably back to retrace

His way to the forest before whose dark, a blazon,
A boy stood; whose mother gasped in alarm,
Whose father approached him with the oddest gaze, then bowed and
                                                                             returned him gently,
Guiding him by the arm?

THE LAUGH

> *… a low iron laugh*
> *Came from afar, a furious epigraph*
> *To what I knew …*
> — Yvor Winters

Perhaps the most subtle act of deception
I ever practiced on myself was when
My father died and I resolved to see my mother on
A regular basis again.

He and I had clashed on most matters
Since my youth, and this had one effect
Of forging a distance between me and Mother,
Not strong enough to reject

His materialism and pragmatic approaches.
I had the idea her last years might be bettered,
Given another chance as a mother, and possibly with
My filial bent unfettered,

I should go less guilt-ridden. Visits to her
Began their regular basis. Phone calls, too.
In the next sixteen years, I trapped myself well in a web
Of obligations you

Could call ridiculous. No deviation
In all those calls and visits, hardly ever.
Nor did I catch her hints 'you needn't be so conscientious.'
But we were both clever

Enough to keep up the pretense until
I at least thought her appreciation
Of my attentions real. To add reality, I doctored
Our exchanges with altercation –

A relationship with bumps. She had
A woman on whom she depended also, a loyal
Soul whom, as Christmas neared, I resolved to give a gift,
And this would seem altogether "royal" –

No, fittingly equal to her services.
After some vague, brief discussion, Mother agreed
It was a good idea. But the amount, disclosed, she thought
Highly excessive. She'd

No hesitation in telling me I was exposed, throwing
Away good money, I couldn't afford. I found
The reaction ugly. I told her all my life I'd felt that we'd
Never been on solid ground.

Since I could never tell when she was teasing or serious –
We'd never communicated. I was cleaved in half
By her responding silence which became an eerie,
Vindictive, prolonged, and savage laugh.

PRECOCITY

People are quite inventive but sometimes so
Weird, far-fetched, I sighed, as I threw down
The *Psychopathia Sexualis* I'd holed up
With for three days at the Muehlebach Hotel,
Instead of visiting a favorite uncle of both
My father and myself.   A friend my age at school (both twelve)
Had lent me the book, saying, "From all I'd heard
You just go in and out – let me know your
Opinion." I couldn't disagree, though first
I'd thought, Why all *these* props and deviousness
To get some pleasure? Then: maybe it's pain
They want. Then: maybe they're alike?
Not for me, I groaned on, returning the book.
Yet, I felt better armed for my first encounter
With a hottie, something wrong in the head.

1940s: HIPSTERS ON A WINTER NIGHT

They could afford to float around in their
Dark-blue formfitting topcoats, in front
Of Optimo cigar store, collars up then
To their DAs, and spin saliva'd blunt

Tales about the broads they laid and those
Impregnable fortresses none could, until
It got cold or late enough for one to rasp
Of a square party they could crash, kept to himself

Like champagne to reach the proper chill. Then off
Like a half-dozen toweled corks they flew
Into the foam and tingles of their lives
To nothing happening there much faster now.

OLD-TIMERS

So, thus, when he died, she hobbled out to the Home
To pull the sheet from his body to be sure
They'd not beaten, whose Polish-army nightmares had frightened her
For decades. No kiss. No tears.

When the last of soil was patted into place,
She let the Siren in herself attest
And, marched from the grave, wailing one foot stuck out. For weeks,
                                                                       no one
Could put that foot to rest.

When she herself was packed off to the Home,
A framed picture of him as a newlywed
Was set to face her, and none was sure why she kept on muttering
Cossacks kept coming to her bed.

LYRIC

If it is true (as a friend of sorts once said)
That toward the end of every person's days
He notices the quality of life
Has changed irrevocably, values based
On less criteria than ever and
Embraced by those his own age, as well as
Younger explorers darting in and out
Of his vocation, why, what can he do,
Without feeling, appearing paranoid,
Except awaken in a darkened space?
He can't judge the size or contents of
(Whether its single chink of light appears
To be above or below his eye-level,
Weak or bright, it makes no difference now,
Since he suspects he has never been here
And so is forced to proceed toward that light
Slowly and by only his own experience)
And so must stumble, provided he does not
Fall fatally, that what he's managing
Bears out the meaning of his kind of life,
And so is brushed by a somewhat troubling pleasure.
And probably he emerges into light
Without his knowing exactly what is taking place,
And wonders what is true and who it was,
Whoever said it might be, and that any of it matters.

FOR BARACK OBAMA, 44TH U.S. PRESIDENT

This, for your first work-day
In the White House, sir;
For if and when you've time,
Inclination, or humor
To skim it. It is mainly
My own need and pleasure,
And it is neither too short
Nor too repetitive. So.

You are a brilliant man,
Tactician, strategist,
Gracious, handsome, and not,
I hope to your God, a martyr
By your own or others' intents,
Nor dependent on miracles,
Unless our freedoms, and
Respect from other nations,

Suggest themselves. For you
Have chosen the public life,
Now you're the helmsman
In a land still
Probably the most free on earth:
Ironically, a land
Free because of its factions,
Splinter groups; their grumblings

Or open hatred for
Each other, a working balance
Or deadlock, as you will.
Every race, religion,
Brand of imbecile,
Or intellect we have.
This has provided an
Uneasy peace for us;

Grounds for power grabs,
Philanthropy, and crime,
But still a peace able
To suffer and outlast
The most corrupt, secretive,
Stupid, cruel, eight-year
Chain gang ever to govern us.
Our apathy helped of course.

The "peace" within our borders
Allowed self-interests and cons
To carry on. Then a man,
Half-white, half-black, mislabeled
Afro-American (which
Had meant black), not what
A good many wanted, with
An Islamic middle name,

No wish for that either
For we had invaded Islam
(Still not sure why), this man,
You, barnstormed the nation with
Courage, restraint, commonsense,
Seemingly endless energy,
Good will. The media, selling
Its soul forever, caved

Like a house of cards. Many feared
Assassination before
His inauguration. He showed
What a feeling thinker and speaker
Could get across. A horde
Of CEOs, bankers, swindlers
Shall mass before your door
To "consult" you. Don't disappoint us.

Sir, you have been left a larger
Inheritance of deceit
To clean up in your role
Than predecessors: unending
War, beleaguered health
Care, pollution, climate
Instability, education,
America's gift for blaming.

Fix what you feel needs most.

PHILOKTETES II

Of course, the wound my serpent had inflicted
Was as offensive in its stench
As it was painful, but then there were my master Herakles's
Bow and arrows could wrench

All birds and animals from flight. Now, as
I grew used to loneliness, I winced
Realizing that I had somehow forgiven Odysseus
And his crew their expedience

Abandoning me on this island. Yet, when they
Returned, I and the whining weapon were needed
To win their War, I saw, at their approach, how the reek
And fear of my revenge impeded;

And what I'd thought was my forgiveness flared
To its former fury. That of course made the cagey
One babble of how they loved me, how surely I must place Greece
Over grievance – so stagey.

He went on about how he'd been filled with misgivings
When they'd trashed me, despite all the accursèd
Dangers of Troy. His cravenness did it, so rarely in character:
Of course, I went. The worst

Thing is to see all sides of everything.

THE ANGEL

The neighbors always knew when spring and fall
Had really settled in, for Lorna and Lon
Liked to sit on their porch more than anything; and always,
After a steady run

Of mild spring days, the angel would appear
On the porch rail and, when the days grew short
And blustered, it vanished. As may have befit an angel, no
One saw it come or depart.

No one knew if Lon or Lorna moved it.
None knew who'd bought it for whom how long ago.
People had ventured guesses. Lon would smile and murmur, "Oh, I
Imagine Lorna'd know."

But something about his cavalier drollness kept
Them all from asking her. Did he believe
In God? Someone once risked. Lon thought. "About as much as I
                                                                             do
In the angel" his reprieve.

A pale gray, ceramic garden ornament,
Six inches high, the angel was formed to sit.
And it played a kind of pipe. Attached to the far end of the rail,
To breeze or storm it submitted.

Some neighbors called it the pair's guardian angel.
Then, after Lorna died, some named it Death.
Lon heard that once; gave the speaker a shrug; then studied the angel
Until tears slipped forth.

In time he seemed unsure now what to do with it,
And fall was on its way. Sometimes he thought
He saw her silhouette form 'round its blank, blind gaze. Sometimes a
                                                                                                dear
Tune she'd used to hum he caught.

INGRES

(1780-1867)

Unquestionably one of the greatest draftsmen
In painting, able to create an aura
Enhancing, intensifying the perfect, under-
lying actuality of the person
Being painted, so that the subject became
The archetype, so to speak, of himself,
Both individual and member of a class,
So each portrait, down to the last detail
Of dress, expression and posture, represented
A culture, by itself; yet, this was colored
By painting only people and the very
Wealthy at that, and the man himself bitched
Constantly that commission begat commission
And, while earning a fortune and meeting important
Figures and making an enviable reputation
Among artists everywhere, he was entertaining
A mockery of himself, being possessed
Above everything else by rank ambition.
There were always at least two or three unfinished
Or unbegun canvases of portraits
Lying about his studio, with more
Commissions arriving. Everyone knew of this,
But Ingres hungered to be the greatest painter
Of his day. In 1827, he'd done
The Apotheosis of Homer, a work
Dear to his heart for its classical theme, its dealing
With ancient Greece, his worship of David

And, later, Raphael. He also painted
A few religious works he likewise cherished.
He constantly complained he had no time
To explore these areas as he had hoped to.
"You know Paris. Well, it has fallen on me.
As soon as I think I have climbed to the top of the abyss,
I see myself fall right back in. Every
Moment is accounted for, all my
Evenings are preceded by dinners arranged
In advance . . . I would prefer the calm of home . . .
Where I forget all my troubles . . . where I
Am happy with the difficulties (of)
My beautiful art, sometimes crowned with my own
Approval…"
    Delacroix, who'd earned his own
Honors and devotees meanwhile, had grown
Along with lesser lights to be Ingres's
Bête noire. The former's themes were, after all,
Heroic; he hadn't invested himself in portraits;
His gift was pervasive.
    Meanwhile, the Marquis
De Pastoret, whom Ingres painted, arranged
An enormous banquet in his honor, with
Four hundred twenty-six guests from the new royal
Family, old aristocracy, various
Academies, and the Universities of Fine
Arts and Interiors — 'the finest names
Of the intellectual aristocracy'
As the press put it; Berlioz produced
A concert with works by Ingres's 'divine'

Gluck and Weber, sung by Del Sarte and
Massol, and performed by former pensioners
Of the Académie de France in Rome.
'So complete was the triumph that, just as Ingres
Himself might have anticipated, it
Provoked ridicule.' Thinking the time right
Now to immerse his talent once again,
In the Ancients and the Classics, he painted
Cherubini and the Muse of Lyric Poetry
In 1842, which the king then purchased,
But which, ironically, served to bring about
His unofficial status as court painter
And produced a virtual avalanche of commissions,
Many for some of the most important models
On the Continent.

    Irony after irony:
Ingres repossessed certain earlier
Altarpieces from various churches, so they
Could be used in Paris; he also commenced
To show his works always in odd groupings:
A portrait alongside a scene from Antiquity
Alongside a religious work, ostensibly
To prove his mastery of more than one
Genre—but this only confused the critics:
Betty de Rothschild side by side with Venus
Anadyomene? Reactions varied
Widely, which might have done Ingres good;
However, while lesser minds praised (Geoffroy:
The Venus was 'particular and strange'

With no particularization; Gautier, over-
extravagant: 'Nothing remains of the marvelous
Painting of the Greeks, but surely if
Anything could give the idea . . . it
Is M. Ingres's painting: the Venus Anadyomene
Of Apelles has been found.'), there firmly stood
Delacroix' fair insistence that he objected
To Ingres's bullying on 'the primacy
Of his own method and the superiority
Of his own school,' and Baudelaire in
1846 put his finger on it:
'Around M. Ingres, whose teachings must inspire
Some kind of fanatical austerity,
Are grouped several men, the best known being
Messrs. Flandrin, Lehmann and Amaury
Duval. But what an immense distance from
Master to students! M. Ingres is still alone in
His school . . . however bizarre and obstinate
(His method) might be, it is sincere, which is
To say, involuntary. Passionate lover
Of Antiquity and its model, respectful servant
Of nature, he makes portraits that rival the best
Roman sculptures.' Delacroix had muttered,
Precipitously perhaps, earlier: '...not the slightest
Logic and no imagination at all.'

Napoleon's 1855 Exposition
Universelle selected four artists
To be exhibited: Ingres, Delacroix,
Vernet, and Decamps (the popular painter of

Lowly genre scenes). Ingres: the reluctant
Participant, whose cooperation was gotten
Only by the promise of a separate room,
The only granted, complete control of its contents
And positionings, and an award of special honors
Guaranteed by Prince Napoleon, the emperor's
Cousin, who was in charge of the event.
The rivalry between Ingres and Delacroix,
Formerly a fact confined to artistic circles,
Became a matter for public debate after
The show: Ingres had caught Delacroix
Leaving the former's turf before Opening;
'Delacroix smiled tightly and excused himself,'
Whereupon Ingres said to an assistant,
"The odor of heresy is surely here."
It should be said Ingres in '46
Had (inadvertently?) created one
Of the most direct, unaffected portraits of
His later career, that of Hortense Reiset—
A masterwork. And the one of Madame
Henri Gonse (1845-52)
Is every bit as excellent.
                Ingres's wife
Madeleine had died in 1849;
His grief was immense: "Everything is finished.
I have her no more, no home, I am broken . . ."
But, by 1851, his ever-consoling
Charles Marcotte had introduced the artist,
Now 71, to a devout spinster
Of 43 who lived with her elderly parents.

The two married, and Delphine managed not
Only to restore Ingres's spirits,
Get him back to painting, but make him utterly
Happy. The Goncourt brothers, after
The 1855 Exposition, naturally
Had their say: '. . . to avoid embarrassing her,
He colored his gray hair brown; evidently
Remained a vigorous husband; on the way home
From the Opéra, the Ingres's carriage was seen
Shaking from all the activity within.'
Nor was that sufficient. They later observed:
'We stopped before dinner, to view the exhibition
On Boulevard des Italiens, to see
The latest painting by M. Ingres . . .
Here, perhaps, is the man who, since
The beginning of time, has most tricked God: he was born
To paint as Newton was born to be a singer!
He has all the talent that determination can give—
That is, hardly any genius and
A talent of sixth order . . . There is not
A morsel of paint on that big canvas.'
The Turkish Bath of 1862—
Along with *The Golden Age* and other classical
Subjects, achieved in quiet retirement—
Proved Ingres's triumph with the human likeness,
The cross he may or may not have at last thought
He'd borne his entire life, as well as mastery
In his lessons from the Ancients and Raphael.

MUNCH

(1863-1944)

> *'I and all my family sat, winter in and winter out, yearning for the Sun. Until Death took them, one by one. I and all my family . . . paced the floor in the grip of mad depression.' (Mostly) he experienced the world as a demonic force which filled him with fear and sadness. He tried to keep its panic-inducing power at bay; it represented the Other to which he was resigned but unable to control . . . At times he attempted a more harmonious relationship with it, but his inborn fear was never far away...*
>
> — P. E. Tøjner, *Munch: In His Own Words*

Being weighed down by family grief was but
One burden. Munch could be said to have borne
All curses save material poverty
That most painters of any time have known;
And also a bout of near-blindness, which
He desperately tried to paint. Ignored by Norway
For many years till, after success in Berlin
And other European capitals,
He returned home, having severed connections
Out of contempt for all their styles of art,
Leaving his rising success in mid-air,
And bought a great expanse of land above
A fjord named Ekely in 1916;
And thirteen years later made useable
Its scattering of ten decrepit barns,
All into studios of different sizes
Where he worked on oils, woodcuts, lithographs,
The oils ranging from small paintings to his
Huge canvases we see today. Ten
Maybe at a time, lined up against

A barn, he'd work on all of them through winter,
In snow boots, dapperly dressed beneath a fine
Coat and fur hat, for hours. The sparse, outlying
Peasantry regarded him as a real
Estate magnate with villas to sell or rent.
His shows, though less, continued to open throughout
Europe, though he kept minimal correspondence
And intervention; his fame went up and down
While he immured himself in art completely,
Surrounding himself with many finished works
In each studio to keep him company
And leaving his radio on continuously
Because of his fear of silence, another hardship.
One could interpolate an ironic, public
Possibility for this: *The Scream,*
His painting of an earlier hallucination,
Had become the one painting everyone
Remembers to this day. This is one
Hazard of any who are artists.
                        Munch
Also suffered from his obsession with women;
Lusted, was jealous, often nagged or rejected,
And refused ever to marry. Alcoholism
Dogged him relentlessly over the years
Till he was confined in Copenhagen, nearly
Paralyzed. Yet even after hos-
pitalization: 'It helped to inspire my painting.'
His still imperiling eye disease; his lifelong
Paranoia about everything, including
The black-humored (though reflection-prompting)

Constant thundering at the tax collectors
For taxing earnings from the sale of paintings
For whose paints, brushes, stretchers, canvases, frames
He'd already been taxed for and paid—
'One doesn't die, one is murdered by one's
Fellow human beings'; solitude
Till he could bear it no longer, when not working—
'I go out to meet friends . . .' (one speculates
On whom 'friends' could have meant) '. . .when we're together,
Their laughter cuts through me like a knife,
And I flee from them…'; fury with Nasjanal-
Galleriet in Oslo for varnishing his pictures:
He felt this prevented them from breathing, 'causing
Them to choke upon their own illusion
Of self-sufficiency… Porosity
Becomes something to strive for—a living, breathing.
Technique. . . varnished surface (is) the opposite—
A strangulated abyss': these all meant suffering.

On the other hand, he'd pleasures, some questionable.
He had incredible resistance and persistence:
From love for his art to casino gambling.
His technique, speed grew legendary, reaching
The world past Norway. He took most care with his
Self-portraits; he dismissed his public image
As of no importance— 'It became something to avoid! …
Paintings should be able to take up the fight
With the sun and the moon!' The paintings became a part
Of nature; his need for larger formats appeared
To liberate him: the distance between the viewer

Was now greater; the larger perspective allowed
The work to enter nature, so he felt.
He permitted birds to defecate on pictures
Left in the snow, painted outside on purpose;
They were left at the mercy of the elements —
Rain, snow, and wind; at times he threw them up
Into the apple trees. A mixture of their merging
With nature and his 'aging painter's indifference.'

From his early painting *The Sick Child* of his dying
Little sister, their grieving mother seated
At her side, which started and continued a storm
Of comment through Europe that Munch himself was ill,
Decadent, 'to be avoided as a model'—
Which naturally led to his being the guiding
Spirit of German Expressionism— to the close
Of his career, this and his whole oeuvre
Achieved for him the fame of paying attention
To each detail in everything he painted;
Enough have said, for instance: 'Each hair on
His sister's head;' also his mentioning
That one line could create a work of art—
Was questionable, say, in contrast to
His painting *The Sun* (1911-16),
But making more sense in *Beach Landscape, Aas-
gaardstrand*, a drawing from 1891
Which used five, maybe six, thin pencil lines
To depict it indelibly.

                    Intensity
Was the chief ingredient that formed a painter,
He said. A corollary of which: 'Whenever
Things are reduced there is a contrapuntal
Intensification'— this was at the core
Of Munch's style: 'taking away in order to
Display.' This truly served his allegiance to surface.
'The depths . . . destroy— the terrible abyss . . .
One drowns, becomes invisible . . . nobody
Notices.'

            At last, we suspect a possible
Monomaniac: persistence is
His dominant characteristic; it contributes
To the controlled intensity of the work,
A kinship with Van Gogh's flow and fervor;
The deprivations Munch subsumed assisted:
The turn away from worldly patronization,
Acclaim, renown— he'd funds himself. He knew
Why he would rather harm himself than others,
Who knew art is the outcome of dissatisfaction
With one's life— his legacy of paintings
And mass of written prescriptions and prohibitions;
Also, the importance of the quest for self-
esteem; 'an openness of spirit (and) lack
Of direction which bordered on dissolution; yet,
Preoccupied with subjects and ideas
For the most part spiritual, intimate, and
Constructive— one who never painted things
He had not experienced.'

                    A man who could end
A tempest of existence, distanced from women
And alcohol, increasingly taking on
The mannerisms of a hermit and
Focused fixedly on his art and self-
disparagement, who wrote late on 'I imagined
Myself making great progress— at once I sensed
A battle to even keep going, to keep
My balance, jumping from stepping stone to stepping
Stone over the abyss.' He also scribbled
Prickly ditties for us:

                         'Oh, my dear judges,
                         Bohemians and pigs —
                         Just what have I done
                         Well, now I shall tell you!
                         I have crapped on a turd.'

ARSHILE GORKY
(1904-1948)

'...came from no place.'
— Willem de Kooning

De Kooning, doubtless his chief painter-friend
(After Gorky achieved some recognition),
Corrected a New York newspaper that claimed
Gorky had learned much from the former: "I had
My formal art education in Holland, from which
I came, but I learned the most, much more, from Gorky…
Gorky came from no place… was self-taught."
'No place' was true, historically: Armenia
Had become East Turkey, through genocide. In Gorky's
Later works, it was the only land
Inspiring him through constant memories
Derived from his youth: love for his mother (his
'Goddess of Aesthetics'); his younger sister
With whom he emigrated to New York
After their mother died in his eleven-
year-old arms, from starvation; Sumerian,
Hittite, Greek, above all Byzantine
Church art and stone carvings, which remained,
Along with silver-craft, Armenian.

Once here, he used to correspond with the sister:
'I am with Cézanne'; later, '…with Picasso.'
He admired Ingres, Miró, for a while Matta,
His second close friend, and once called a picture
In de Kooning's studio 'very good.' A relationship

With Stuart Davis ended when Davis took
To socialism during the Depression
WPA handouts. Coming 'from no place'
Came to mean, during the 30s and 40s,
Rejecting Cubism; Picasso's love of 'straight
Line' and 'urban' art; Surrealism, after
Breton claimed him 'the eye-spring' of that movement.
Soon after, Schapiro, even Greenberg, came
To admire him; then, Rosenberg as well.
Six years after arriving at Ellis Island,
Gorky said, '…real artists, of course, care not
What they sell any more than where they are.
If a painting of mine … does not please me, I
Care not if all the great masters approved it…
They would be wrong. How could there be anything
Fine in my painting unless I put it there
And see it?' That was 1926.

To his life's end in 1948
He mourned, however, for Armenia,
Its landscapes, people, culture. And he talked,
As if out of two mouths, aesthetics also:
(1939)— '… as I oppose
Anarchy in politics, I oppose
Anarchy in Art… (It) negates aesthetic
Art… Unrelenting spontaneity
Is chaos… Quality is not the result
Of abandon.' (1942)— 'Drawing
Is the basis of art. A bad painter cannot draw
But one who draws well can always paint…

Drawing … develops in him the precision of
Line and touch. This is the path toward masterwork.'

Abstraction had come into its own: coming
'From no place' included his hate for American
'Insensitivity, lack of feeling, love
For technology, ignorance of art traditions,
And worship of superficial originality.'
Coming 'from no place' also may have meant
That every time he saw this field or that
Forest or mountain, it reminded him
Of one in Khorkom, where he was born, Vosdanik
Adoian, or Van where he moved when six,
Or Aght'amar in Lake Van, with the 'finest
Church carvings, and in the world's first Christian country.'
Coming 'from no place' also recalled Julien
Levy, his first American dealer: "One
Day you will be with Gorky." He had neither
Fear nor contempt for influence. To feel
The worth of his art, Gorky needed to wed
Armenian images worked into abstractions
With specific European technical approaches.

After a burned-down studio where 30 paintings
Perished, colostomy from cancer, and
Broken neck and painting arm from an auto
Wreck, in rapid succession, he hung himself
In 1948. His reputation
By virtue of that and beauty made its way
And, coming from soul and skill alone, retains its laurels.

LESTER YOUNG
(1909-1959)

> *...surprising that the heated arguments in the 1930s and early 1940s on the relative merits of Young and Hawkins were not even more violent. Young's playing was surely as revolutionary for the time as Parker's was later— in some respects even more so, since Young was not part of a highly publicized movement as was Parker and explored his paths in solitude.*
> — Don Heckman, *Downbeat*, 1963

> *In his last records I hear an unspeakable sadness— an actual pessimism that is rarely to be found in the art of the American Negro up to now. The existence of this quality is not susceptible to rigorous demonstration in prose, but it's there for anyone who can hear.*
> — Louis Gottlieb, *Jazz: A Quarterly of American Music*, ed. Ralph Gleason, 1959

Goodbye, Porkpie Hat

Sensitivity and intransigent in-
dependence. Lifelong anxiety that his color
Consigned him to damnation. As a boy,
He went to a service in a white church:
He and his father, black, took seats in the rear
While a fire-and-brimstone preacher informed those
Wishing to be saved to come up front to the mourners'
Bench, but the bench and salvation were reserved
For whites. Only close to his death, consuming
A fifth of whiskey and two dozen beers, nightly
In his almost bare room at the Hotel Alvin,
Staring outside, tenor sax in his lap,
Absently running his fingers over the pads,
Gazing down on Birdland often played at;

Sometimes attended by Elaine, a young
Woman friend who looked in on him daily
And cared for him, who scarcely ate but drank,
His outer garb was an almost ankle-length
Black coat and broad-brimmed porkpie hat
(His signature outfit for more than two
Decades), she and Manhattan's jazz priest
The Reverend John Gensel, and the jazz-
loving psychiatrist Dr. Luther Cloud
Who visited at times, managed to drive
Out Young's fear of damnation.

               His helping his
Cousin Sport to escape a Southern lynch mob,
When they were teens, had also helped ingrain
A deep mistrust of whites from booking agents,
Club owners, record producers to practically
All of them. To an interviewer he said,
Late on in his 49 years, "They want every
Negro to be an Uncle Tom or Uncle
Remus or Uncle Sam, and I can't make it.
You just fight for your life, that's all. . ." So much
For sensitivity? No. Lester wore quite
An armor, becoming with the years a legend:
Besides the coat and hat, he had a long,
Flat, high-yaller mummy face which spoke
Its own language: "get bruised" (to fail), "get straight"
(Succeed), "big eyes, nice eyes" (approval), "feel
A draft" (feel tension), "Ding-dong" (bored with a question),
"Can Madam burn?" (Can your wife cook?), "zoomer" (sponger),

"His left people" (a pianist's left hand),
"Bing and Bob" (the police), "hat" (a woman);
Basie was "Groundhog," Harry Edison "Sweets,"
Buddy Tate "Moon;" often anyone,
Of either sex, found his name preceded
By the word "Lady," as in Lady Day.

Jimmy Rowles observed, "...he was quiet... unfailingly
Polite. He almost never got mad. If
He was upset, he'd take a small whisk broom
He kept in his top jacket pocket and sweep
Off his left shoulder." Tate remarked, "With Basie. . .
He had a little bell he kept on the stand
Beside him. Whenever someone goofed, he rang it."

In '44, after ignoring repeated
Draft notices, Lester at the Plantation
Club, West Coast, was filming *Jammin' the Blues*,
A documentary directed by Gjon Mili
Of *Life*; a hiply dressed listener, who
Clearly admired the band, bought drinks for Young
And the musicians, and, at the evening's close,
Flipped out his FBI badge and served
Young and Jo Jones with their induction papers.
"Can you imagine that," Young murmured to Tate,
"And I thought he was such a nice Lady."
Pianist John Lewis, around then:
"Young was an extremely gentle, kind,
Considerate person, always concerned about
The underdog." Dozens have echoed this. . .

The deaths of friends and relatives depressed him
Deeply. After years of estrangement from
His father, a musician who'd raised three sons
To read music and learn their instruments,
To play in a family band and make their livings
(He'd whipped Lester for defiantly refusing
To read one note; the boy then fooled his father
For a while, having a fabulous ear and memory),
He drove for days to visit his dying parent.

(Bobby Scott, a pianist who met Young in the early '50s and became one of his closest friends for the duration of the latter's life, wrote a testimony to their intimacy as fellow traveling-musicians, *The House in the Heart*, which appeared in *Jazzletter*, Sept. 1983. The following is an abbreviated selection of extracts from this: "...I came to think his was the exquisite loneliness that comes of a splendid type of isolation ... More players imitated him than were stoked by him. Once, told of a player who 'plays exactly like you' was even called the Something Prez (a nickname), Lester said, 'Then who am I?'... He was influenced more by solos by the Louis Armstrong of the 1920s (than by) his fellow tenor players. Prez didn't arpeggiate in the style of his age. His was a more horizontal linear expression, more in keeping with the approach of a trumpeter, trombonist, or adventurist singer. That distinction is the key to his heavy influence on later players ... Prez was less harmonic than Coleman Hawkins. His preoccupation with the pentatonic scale sang more of his Mississippi folk roots than it did of his later big-city life. It evoked a country preacher more than a streetwise tart. Peculiar it is, too, for it makes less use of the blues than it does rural folk elements ... I am always amazed at how well Prez wears. His expression is not one of *immediate* importance, like Charlie Parker's was, nor so energetic in the rhythmic sense. (Bird suffered terribly from rhythm sections that were a decade behind him in understanding.) Bird was subjective and biting; Prez, more sedate and objective ... Lester was very aware of how people broke hearts with their tongues. A man misjudged as often as Prez was, and offended so easily, would know about that. Accordingly, his own observations were couched in 'unknown' terms, that he might not give offense. I saw it as very responsible behavior … The quiet that surrounded and covered Lester was of a contemplative nature and origin. If he allowed me to 'divert' him, he did it out of an interest in, and a love for, me. He didn't need diversion. Small things could and would draw his interest and attention.")

His gentleness had a shrewd side as well.
Deathly afraid of needles (unlike his friend
Billie Holiday and others), in advance
Of a spinal tap he was ordered to undergo
Before induction, he prepared himself
With home-brewed sauce, result of which he spent
Three days in a mental clinic, winding up
In Fort McClellan, Alabama. Soon
His C.O. noticed his inattention, and questioned.
Young confessed he was high and showed the man
Some pills he carried; a search of his quarters yielded
More pills and marijuana joints. He said
He'd get feeling good and forget to hide the stash,
Adding, "I've never harmed anyone." Justice
Got on his case. A general court martial
Met, and his defense counsel, Major Grimke,
Did his best for his client, considering Young
Admitted charges brought. Grimke called only
One defense witness, the accused himself,
Directing the court's attention sympathetically
To the gap between Young's and the soldier's life,
Implying the former should not have been inducted.
He was asked how long he'd been using narcotics;

Replied; was asked if he could train without them;
Replied, "No, sir. Because I tried it, sir.
I tried it truthfully." Grimke convinced
The five-officer panel that Young would fail
As a soldier. Still, he got the maximum
Punishment: a year's hard labor after
Dishonorable discharge.

                Years before,
Praise had cascaded from Goodman, Basie, Hammond.
Then there was Fletcher Henderson who'd hired him,
And after the band's whole sax section had buzzed him
And Fletcher's wife Leora had managed to wake
"Their lodger" each morning, escorting him down
To their basement to play Coleman Hawkins's records
So he could learn his predecessor's style,
Lester, unresponsive, politely stated,
"I had in mind what I wanted to play,
And I was going to play that way. This is
The only time someone told me to play
Differently than I wanted." In accord,
Fletcher stood by his protégé, but outbursts
Were tearing the band apart— Hawkins was
The first great tenor stylist in all jazz—
And Fletcher told his crew he'd let Young go
"Because he'll never have peace, staying with you.
But I'll tell you this: he can outplay you, you
And you. And you're going to hear about him."
Aside from Lester's style and way with time,
He'd learned in K.C.'s Reno Club in '36

To hold his horn cocked sideways, his head bent
At an angle precisely opposite. This, he claimed,
Was needed because the bandstand was small,
So crammed, this was the only way to play.
So be it. Nonetheless, it became one more
And perhaps his most lasting eccentricity
Or, rather, his persona's. Sensitivity?
Attention-getting? Independence? So?
The younger generation's tenor players,
Eager, Moore, so many tilted their axes
Likewise, part of the reverence Lester inspired.
The sole player who best emulated Lester,
And after many years brought both their styles
To a point Prez might have applauded, was Stan Getz.

He'd tried drums first as a New Orleans youngster,
Taken with drummers on the music trucks.
Drummers normally held the left stick
With all five fingers; the right, between the fore-
finger and thumb. Lester gripped the right stick
Between fore- and middle fingers. This his father
Tolerated perhaps since the right sounds issued…
He listened to Jimmy Dorsey and especially
Frankie Trumbauer. But the latter used
A C-melody sax, which Young insisted
Led to his own tone on tenor later.
He could play all Trumbauer's tunes and solos
By heart. He also loved the clarinet—
Metal, however—till his death, and played it.
In 1928, he made his final

Instrumental choice, the tenor, with Bronson's
Band, playing Kansas and Nebraska— "As
Soon as I wrapped my mouth around it, I knew
It was for me. Alto was too high."

Hawkins's thick and, above all, bold
Attack and total knowledge of the horn,
As well as enviable inventiveness,
Was followed by many then and still, to name
Some: Webster, Davis, Thompson, Rouse, Rollins;
But each contributing brilliancies his own.
Young, well-known by now as Prez (Pres-
ident of the tenor), so dubbed by Lady Day:
Both nicknames stuck for these long-time platonic
Lovers. His sound: vibrato-less except
For rhythmic tricks; air-filled even with fierce
Attacks at faster tempi. Hawkins was openly
Emotional; Lester, cool, tentative, floating.
The Hawk drove home the beat; Prez frequently
Hung behind it, with lengthy, winding phrases
Which might ignore bar or chorus divisions.
Hawk usually played long runs of notes;
Prez hit some; bent, implied others; and often
Would fill even his faster choruses with
Weird, unexpected silences. Balliett,
Good critic, amused by quipping, "He would sooner
Have gone into another line of work
Than place a note conventionally." But it
Worked every time. A paradox came clear
That, though Prez's solos mimicked "lazing,"

He could, due to halts, timed daringly,
Swing as well as Hawk— often more so.

A final tableau of the way these two titans
Pursued their art might well be of a recording:
Despite that Young and Holiday were ill
And would die four months apart in '59,
Billie, hunched in a chair before her mike;
Lester, standing up only to solo and play
Obbligati behind her—a studio gambit
With *Fine and Mellow*, a blues, of course, with group
Including Hawk and Webster at their strongest,
Assembled by Balliett and Nat Hentoff,
Exploded CBS-TV's *Sunday Jazz
Spectacular*, of which the latter wrote,
"Prez was slumped in a chair, but when it came
Time for his solo, somehow he managed to stand…
And then he blew the sparest, purest blues
Chorus I've ever heard." In the control room,
Hentoff, techies wept openly….

              In the Alvin
Cubbyhole, Lester kept the minimum:
Clothes, sax, booze, porkpie hat on a wall nail,
A picture of his parents on the dresser.
Elaine brought him a little food each day
And took him for a walk when he was able.

FALLING

> *In old age, stenosis of the lumbar spine*
> *may lead to lower leg and foot neuropathy*
> *causing a possibly complete lack of physical balance.*

A good five decades back, I'd gone with friends
To watch their university's performance
Of Beckett's *Godot*, where, at the intermission,
I took advantage to stretch in the rear alcove,
Where some of the crowd smoked, drank, chatted.
Standing near a circle of five or six,
I watched a younger man exit the restroom
Hurriedly and striding at the bell's
Summons back to the performance, he ac-
cidentally, brushed the side of an older fellow,
One of the circle, and moved on without
A word or breaking his pace. I saw the brushed
Man fall backward stiffly, straight as he'd stood,
And strike his occipital skull, cabby's cap
Knocked wide, on polished tiles. Glancing
At him, en route to my seat, I caught the rest of his circle close and
                                                                     stoop
Around him, and regained my seat, drenched in the sight and fear.

These days, short walks, with my cane –
Office, helping unload groceries from the car,
Exchanging brief tidings in our halls
Or basement-laundry with tenants, staff – but even
In my rooms, carpeted, that I know well,
I have my five or six falls a year –

A slide on old newspapers, a grandchild's toy,
Tripping on wastepaper baskets left jutting
In front of furniture, a soapy floor.
Outdoors, I don't dare look save where I step;
And, should I pause to cast a look abroad,
I often feel a helping hand's support.
But I've no guarantees. A turn halfway 'round
May end in a fall. I scan the ground. I seldom
Lift my gaze save when seated or prone…
If I sense myself falling, I let my cane fly,
Go limp, shield skull, forearm fending off.

A COMFORTER

Job

He has a problem.
He is confronted
By two different
Ideas (one
For each of two
Poems to be written).
He refused to discard
Either, though
The pleasure and pain
Obtained from writing
One, may reduce
Or supplant the desire
To write the other.
Anyway, which
Should he write first:
The first or the second?

Comforter

The second. If he
Writes the second
First, he'll write
The first second.

A WORKPLACE

A first-rate editor, a family man,
Yet so reticent about everything
Else about him (modest? attention-seeking?) – what was this room
                                                         he'd
Keep on mentioning?

He did so about once every six months,
A surprise always, his reason never clear,
He'd give a fleeting glare, but at last I learned he kept a cot
And his old Royal there.

He'd not say where it was, but every year
Or so he'd rent a new retreat. In a burst
Of recklessness I asked, "What for?" He snapped, "A woman…
                                                         a story…
Whichever one comes first."

A FAREWELL
Robert Stock (1923-1981)

He'd not wanted to come, he'd not wished us
To see how slow his walk had grown, a sort
Of shambling; the self-assured manner: a downturned, apologetic
Gaze as we left the airport.

Was it he was afraid his former supple,
Inexorable brilliance and logic would
Make him seem a freak to us now that a failing body
Belied his fortitude?

What was it? We embraced him, seized the valise,
And drove him home for the agreed two weeks,
Where he rambled of poems and loved ones, and told travel stories to
                                      our children,
But his glass of gin would speak.

Also, chain-smoking with his emphysema;
Angina, glaucoma, *they'd* get in a word –
And guilt, too, had a place. There was more than a touch of
                                      showmanship in it,
A dash of the absurd.

Drink, sleep, drink: that was about all it came to –
Blear journey from where to where. He *must* abhor it.
Remembering all he'd done, all he'd inspired, and still spoke for –
Well, we must love him for it.

What had it meant, his visit? We may have wondered
As we drove to the airport now. Few words could be found.
When at Security, our Orpheus turned and gazed, we knew
We would be left behind.

THE ARK OF NEWARK

Kea Tawana, good woman of Newark,
Prodigiously gifted, very strong, willful,
Who'd built her house over a sizable truck;
Tough, optimistic, sociable, who worked
On construction sites to earn her bread;

Learned joinery, was able to gather timbers
For her own labors, judging the ones needed
By herself, from abandoned buildings, carting,
Cataloguing and stacking on unclaimed,
Vacant lots alongside where she lived,

Got the idea in 1973,
When she was nearing forty, to start planning
To build an Ark, on which she began work
Some nine years later. What Kea completed
All alone a few years after became,

In a short time, a well-loved local landmark:
The framework of her biblically conceived
Vessel stood 80-feet-long and at least
Three stories high. For many blocks around,
Appreciative neighbors gazed, admired,

And guessed for many days and nights just whom
Or what and where the land-bound ship would bear;
Its fame spread like a tide. Nevertheless,
Its dominating presence brought the dove
Of Newark's angry Department of Engineering

Just months thereafter, to bring tidings to Kea
The Ark was unsafe and had to be demolished.
Kea's response was to post atop her craft
A large and clearly visible plywood sign:
"Help! The City wants to destroy this Ark—

Call (three numbers followed): Tell them to stop it!"
In spite of court cases and campaigns by
Numerous public figures, authorities won:
The Ark was ordered moved out of Newark
Or faced destruction. No site could be found.

At length, its maker herself took a chain saw
To it. But that failed to appease the city
Goons: they harassed her further by official
Threats to destroy her very home. With time,
They relented enough to tell her: "Tow it elsewhere!"

JUDAS AHASVERUS

        (*Seringueiros*, early 20th century)

From far in the *sertão*, the drought-ridden
Wastes of northeastern Brazil, starved rubber tappers
Made a pilgrimage to fell the trees
Near the headwaters of the great Purús River,
Gathering second-rate *caucho*, suffering
A like fate to their countrymen's who hauled
Seringa, drawn from cuts in deep-jungle
Stands in eternal dusk. Both types of dupes
Led nomadic lives. Those near the Purús,
Exiles from bad to worse, soon contracted
All manner of illness; lost their sense of time
And place in soggy flatlands out to horizons
Facing more of the same; moved on perforce
In search of unfelled groves, just as the others
Drifted on through hidden forest recesses—
Rubber and hope for wages enough to leave
Their nightmare rounds kept them just alive,
Enslaved to rubber traders and ignored
By Rio government thousands of miles southeast.
Their lives nevertheless found expression:
All Holy Week represented for them
The torturing sameness of a doomed existence
Made up of identical days of penury,
Permanent bleak environment stretching forth
To the year ahead, except for Holy Saturday.

Elsewhere these seven days were spent in lands
Where activity stopped— depopulated streets,
Shut businesses, deserted roads, flickering
Candles, silence save for voices praying
Faintly, and meditation, identification
With God's prodigious sorrow. These seven days,
For others, seemed more significant than all
Their days of happiness.

                For rubber tappers,
Though, in Amazonas, their pain-filled,
Anonymous, God-forsaken year, including
Holy Week, except for Holy Saturday,
Was an unchanging Via Dolorosa
Without beginning or end. But quite unlike,
Say, the Italians and others, who abuse
God's goodwill by enjoying colorful outrage,
Rebellion, blasphemy, the *seringueiros*
Resigned themselves to misfortune the following way:

Come Holy Saturday, they punished themselves
For despised ambition that brought them to this pass
To be the pawns of deceiving contractors:
Now, on this single joyous day, they resorted
To their pageant where they identified with Judas.
The fathers threw themselves into deception,
Aided by youngsters in ecstasies of laughter,
Who searched for loose straw and discarded pieces
Of filthy clothing, which they stuffed and sewed
Into a life-sized Judas doll, with arms

And legs outstretched, and mounted on
A pole in the communal square; a straw-
filled ball was impaled atop the pole, distinctive
Cruel lines were drawn thereon with charcoal—
Mock torture so tragic, so close to reality,
That the eternally damned figure might seem to have been
Resurrected at the same time as Christ—
Convincing these resentful believers by
Its imaged misery and horrid agony.
A father then tore off his hat and tossed
It onto Judas's head, while all the children
Shrank back with a cry, seeing perhaps portrayed
In the sinister figure the likeness of their parent.
One writer assessed the sight as 'bringing to mind
The Damned as painted by Michelangelo.'
Dolorous triumph: revenge upon themselves…
Yet insufficient.

    A waiting raft on the bank
Received the frightening icon, affixed to its stern.
A bag of stones was tied about the shoulders;
A useless pistol or knife, jammed in its belt,
And given strange recommendations, nonsensical
Advice, Judas was pushed by one of the elders
Into the rushing river.

    Thus, Judas-made-
Ahasverus sailed with the current, shot at
But still upright, mile after mile, by tappers.
Other Judases on their rafts joined him:

A long flotilla downstream, almost endless—
The open sea its destination perhaps,
Maybe the world at large—mocking in all
Directions, bobbing with currents, birds scattered
In fear; amphibians, fish diving ever
Deeper; men on shore, furious, frightened,
Making the sign of the cross, cocking their rifles,
Judases finally bowing or falling free
From the gunfire, curses, and exorcisms.
Perhaps they convened in some huge, quiet backwater
Or out at sea in the caressing doldrums,
Those that remained afloat, the motionless
Stares of their false eyes crossing, and their vestments
Flailing tattered in the breeze, the distant outcries,
"Begone, wretch!" echoing down twenty centuries.

THE PRISONER POET
for Adele Mosonyi

They had been told to treat him with consideration. So, after they'd pushed him into the cell and locked the door, it opened after a few minutes and a magic marker with fairly broad tip was tossed in and once again the door was locked.

He grasped the idea quickly, and after a few minutes began to write a poem, starting as high up as he could on one wall. A short rest, and then another beneath it. And so on, so that by the end of day he was both tired and somewhat satisfied. Meals were slipped in through slots in the walls at floor level that opened and shut at random.

The next day after breakfast he began afresh, and the next day and the next, until he either needed a new marker, for which he knocked, or all the walls were filled with poetry. One slightly malicious among his captors threw in a ladder one day so the poet could write from the very top of the walls if he so wished. And of course he did; he wanted to preserve the poems below. So much so that he finally covered the whole ceiling as well with his flow of verses. The same captor then slipped in a note suggesting he write on the floor; and there was even one window they never opened, which let in the light until it, too, was written on. And so it went. His captors installed electric bulbs at irregular intervals and positions on all sides of his quarters, keeping them small so he would have the most space on which to write and still be able to sleep. Once, he did feel his way around to try to find the window he had written over so many times, but he either couldn't locate it or had to stop because his hands ached and were black and blue from pounding, since he imagined the window couldn't be shattered; and, in any case, if he kept pounding he would injure his hands so that he couldn't write.

Now, what could they do for him? It was agreed he would be supplied with markers of several colors, simultaneously, so he would be free to choose which colors to use on different days or even the same day, if he'd filled the spaces over which he wrote. By now he'd become ambidextrous, and also was possessed by the growing feeling he was less and less subject to gravity and could with no physical support, if he inclined, which he did not, write in any position, even upside down, as he now was able. He could write free-fall verse, even calligrams, which the spacing of the electric lights sometimes tempted him to try.

It all went rather well for more than a year. The poet had never had so much time in which to compose. He'd never had the opportunity to see all his verses at the same time, and even in chronological order for he lost track of the sequence in which he'd thought them written, or was forced to write over them. One day he might feel he had produced some of the world's finest *terza rima*; another day he'd discover that the beauty of a fragment written upon another made him feel an epic forming or at least the longest sonnet sequence ever managed; epigrams alternated with villanelles, blanks vied with rhymed couplets. He even tried writing in different tongues, for he'd dabbled in at least three, or he would mix them up in the same poem.

He felt actually happy for the first time or at least truly fortunate, for some shred of his critical faculty remained. Since he slept well, whether on the floor, wall, or ceiling, he could tell which surface his best or worst poems now rested on and whether poetry uplifted or depressed—and many poems, he was sure, had long since been written upon by their successors. He slept well, he thought. After some days, during which his captors heard no sound from the cell and deduced his food trays were, like the pullmans of a train, lined up within, and guessed by now he had tried and possibly succeeded in covering himself with writing, the door was opened and a sonogram specialist, a phrenologist, and at last a priest with a working knowledge of magic entered the cell to see what was what. But the cell had wholly to be demolished before they could bring themselves to believe that they had found him.

EVENINGS WITH HOWARD NEMEROV, 1960

One of the very few to write how much
He liked certain poems in my first book,
He would climb our stairs each time slowly and with a tight-lipped
Smile, a reticent look,

Almost as though he thought he'd be turned away.
A lean, handsome man in a loose, long,
Expensive suede jacket, scarf tossed 'round throat, his firm handshake
Would always precede the strong,

Low voice that would open our evenings up
With such remarks as "Well, I'm forty now"
Or "though you have a point, I simply can't agree about that comma
In the last thing I sent you."

Dinners were a quick, relished affair,
Mostly in silence, and then it would begin:
Besofa'd, shoes off, matching glass for glass, and his slow drawl
On oblivion toward oblivion,

(While noting pretty sights along the way).
Our only fully-credentialed man of letters
By 1960 as it grew late, not one below-
The-belt-attack on betters

Or inferiors: he always put them all
In the best light. Once, I asked him why
He'd defend his most obnoxious critic. He said, "Why not?" with a
                                                                             smile

Vulnerable, sly.

At last he'd rise, the perfect gentleman,
Shoulder his jacket, try a few steps, stiffen,
Extend his hand as though from far away, and murmur, tired,
"Next time in hog heaven?"

MEMORY OF TED WEISS RETIRED IN PRINCETON

So here we are, friends, more than forty years,
On a dirt road past Einstein's Institute,
Sun blazing, no bench, shade tree, level rock for you to rest,
Still worse, our troubleshooting,

Our prickly pastime of deploring the present
Poetry scene, its latest foibles. You are
Now eighty, plagued by Parkinson's, and though the way
To your house isn't far,

Your brow's beads of sweat and the rising edge
Of anger in your voice, evaluating
The very writers you'd taught, published, or helped, they hold me here.
Is it the wisest thing,

Old fellow, to leave you standing here, not even
A hat, let's make for the car, drive back? You totter
On with thin-lipped, sour smile, mantled in satisfaction at our
Impatience, as always, utter-

Ly firm benevolence underlies annoyance,
By giving a sound, deft, critically searing
Whack to those who've strayed, but tactfully and protectively
For them, beyond their hearing.

SONG OF DECLINE

Nothing significant happens anymore,
Or seems to, or else we don't remember it.
Each day we spend time with our store
Of images, some canceled out of habit;

Then, others appear. When they do, from far back
In our lives: regardless from which angle
We study them, they always lack
Reality. Those recent tangle

With one another, in the process
Making demands; we've little faith
We could ever satisfy them. Is
This the mind's work? Just distraction from death?

The mind slows down because of this question.
Thus, we have one cause: to celebrate
Worries that we wait and wait, our waiting aimless, worthless.
Other than that, we exist only to wait.

DIMINISHMENT

Earthshakers? Hardly necessary. Perhaps
Sledgehammers, phone calls. A steady, light tapping.
Demolition. Maybe the reconstruction
For that matter. Maybe the settling of
Affairs, involving the bureaucrats, which,
Though it progresses, like most legal matters
Advances deviously, at a snail's pace or
Insidiously pernicious, like multisyllabic
Nouns in a paragraph of one- and two-
syllable words, because they distract from telling.
Possibly it's allergies? Maybe it's junk
You take for them. Or maybe just suppression
Of fear of something catastrophic in
The future, at a time of which you are
Disconcertingly more aware than of
The event itself which may or may not happen.
Maybe an omen, inevitable,
Or something felt at last that has been going
On for years and has prevented you
From planning very much. You are exhausted.
Maybe this will protect you from yourself?
As you lose ground, the disappointment's less
Because you can bear less. That's the reward.

GETTING IT RIGHT

> ... *the humility specific to a vocation for poetry,*
> *i.e., the terrible disavowal of experiences and know-*
> *ledges for which one does not yet have the words.*
> — John Logan (in a review of Isabella Gardner)

I don't believe *humility* is what
A poet learns – indeed, any of us –
Frustration, fear, self-deception might serve as well or better,
From having to dismiss,

Not having felt deeply enough, whatever chance
May visit on him next or, say, the ground
He stands on any moment, simply because at that moment
Or shortly he hasn't found

The language to relate it. Nor am I sure
I shouldn't *disavow* these very lines
That I am writing now, who can't know what they'll mean, until
The final word confines

Them all and opens up a meaning, or
Confusion. Terrible, yes, to have to wait
(How long?) to know what something said, but that's not what we do:
We find and delegate

Certainty to doubt, with every
Explanation we birth – which cancels out
Our previous. Often, having no more is what convinces
The words we use are right.

GONESBERG

d. April 1997

First caught <u>your</u> show at Walter the Waiter's bash,
Prompting, with boredom's wings, Corso's scowl:
("Well, time to do it") and off the clothes came; his briefs kept on,
He more the howl.

How many years did I defend Part I
Of *Howl* and little else you'd write? I really
Should forget. The worst was your *Collected*, America's thickest,
More padded than Creeley's,

Whose lines ran short at least. But Gonesberg was
No third-rate Vietnam:
Performance poetry, media gamesmanship, Tantra, Gay Rights –
Each word sweetened to rhyme.

You put your queer shoulder to Mary Jane
To legalize her, or was that just a chance
To clog the cogs of Congress? One needed only that a Vendler parse
Yid wit for it to prance

Forth, suit and tie, and fake the teaching bit.
You led American verse into a slum.
If we'd one global household-word poet, you were he.
Good show, dharma bum.

AND THEN...

Turning down St. Placide, hurrying toward
Harmonia Mundi, a record store, I was
Stopped short gently but firmly by an ab-

solutely stunning, young black woman, wearing
A summery, yellow-rose print, taking me
(Near eighty) by surprise. So much so

That she held me with a neutral, steady gaze,
Saying in softly modulated English:
"Sir, would you care to join me? I shall show you

The most marvelous time of your life." I didn't even
Blink. Knowing I'd been disarmed, she went
On matter-of-factly: "I was married to a kind,

Wonderful man in Mauretania once.
We came here, lived for a few years, menial work.
And then I saw him at a café with a good-looking,

Equally young, white man, engaged in talk,
Laughing, enjoying each other. I let it pass.
I saw them again, some weeks later, same

Café, and questioned him that night. We always
Loved each other, always honest together.
He told me the man was paying him good money

And no danger. And we could use the money.
Sometime later, my husband took sick.
To make it brief: he died eventually,

Here in Paris. He'd stopped seeing the fellow.
My husband died of AIDS. Of course, I caught it."
She'd shown no emotion—precise and steady.

I wondered: Why me? Because I was old?
Because I seemed harmless? Why me?
She beamed a lovely smile, thinking perhaps,

Sensing perhaps my thoughts. . .
                    "You're admirable,"
I smiled, palm on her shoulder. "But right now,

I've not the time you merit." "Really, my friend,
I can show you the best time you've ever had."
"I suspect you could, my dear." I hurried on.

NOTES

Judas Ahasverus. *Seringueiros:* Rubber tappers from the region and time specified, which bred unrelieved poverty, because of aridity, no irrigation, sparse game, and barely a link with the capital Rio thousands of miles distant. These conditions, however, provided knowledge of surrounding terrain; sophistication which, while recognizing basic Christian iconographic components, tended to confuse meanings and identities. News, such as the advent of the rubber industry far inland, was sketchy. *Caucho:* Rubber from felled trees. *Seringa:* First-rate rubber from cuts in the bark of rain-forest trees.

The Prisoner Poet. Parisian painter Adele Mosonyi did a diptych in 2008 (acrylics and Japanese paintbrush marker) showing her conception of this prose piece, exhibited it with the text, and presented me with the much-appreciated gift of her painting.

BIOGRAPHICAL NOTE

David Galler. Born in NYC in 1929, David Galler went to the Horace Mann School where he developed a side interest in jazz, becoming a drummer and subbing with Charlie Parker once when Max Roach was unavailable. Parker asked Galler to play a waltz (which he did). Shifting to poetry, he began by translating French and Spanish surrealist poets of the early 20th century and trying his own hand at this genre when he was in his late teens. Later, he apprenticed himself to Pound's example and then to William Carlos Williams. By 1959, he was devoting his efforts chiefly to what is known as formal verse. He has been writing in this vein ever since. Many of the poems in this book treat of what the author has called "my post-end-of-life crisis." His range and variety of themes is prolific. His son, Robert Jurgrau, borrowed the much annotated manuscript from his father to help prepare this volume. Today, David spends his time reading, watching movies – he particularly enjoys French ones with Isabelle Huppert – and thinking about new topics to write about.

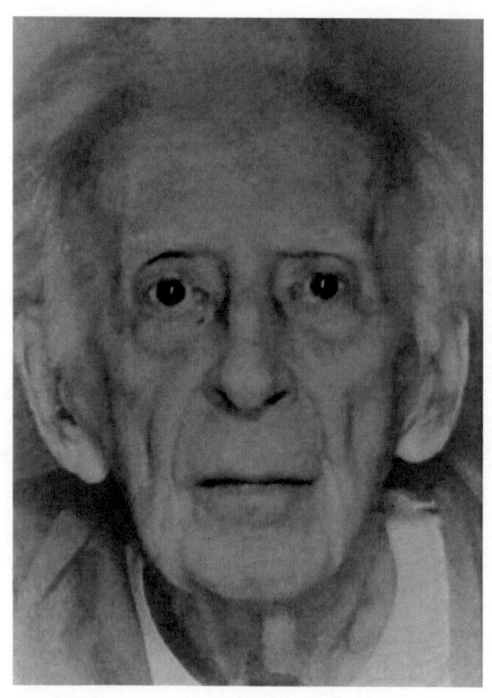